Reading/Writing Companion

Mc
Graw
Hill

mheducation.com/prek-12

Send all inquiries to:
McGraw Hill
1325 Avenue of the Americas
New York, NY 10019

ISBN: 978-1-26-572351-4
MHID: 1-26-572351-6

Printed in the United States of America.

3 4 5 6 7 8 9 LMN 26 25 24 23 22

A

Welcome to WONDERS!

We are so excited about how much you will learn and grow this year! We're here to help you set goals for your learning.

You will build on what you already know and learn new things every day.

You will read a lot of fun stories and interesting texts on different topics.

You will write about the texts you read. You will also write texts of your own. You will do research as well.

You will explore new ideas by reading different texts.

Each week, we will set goals on the My Goals page. Here is an example:

I can read and understand texts.

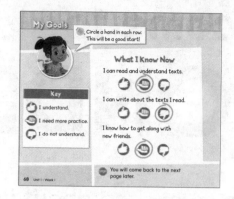

As you read and write, you will learn skills and strategies to help you reach your goals.

You will think about your learning and sometimes circle a hand to show your progress.

Here are some questions you can ask yourself.

- Did I understand the task?
- Was it easy?
- Was it hard?
- What made it hard?

It is okay if I need more practice. The most important thing is to do my best and keep learning!

If you need more help, you can choose what to do.

- Talk to a friend or teacher.
- Use an Anchor Chart.
- Choose a center activity.

At the end of each week, you will complete a fun task to show what you have learned.

Then you will return to your My Goals page and think about your learning.

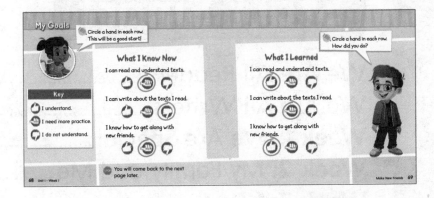

Start Smart

We Are All Readers...6

We Are All Writers...8

Week 1: We Are Special 10

Week 2: My Family and Me 28

Week 3: I Can! 46

Unit 1 Take a New Step

The Big Idea

What can we learn when we try new things?............64

Week 1 • Make New Friends

Build Knowledge 66
My Goals 68

Literature Big Book *What About Bear?*

Respond to the Big Book 70
Character 72
Analyze the Text 74

Shared Read "I Can"

76

Paired Selection "How to Be a Friend"

Analyze the Text 82

Shared Read "Can I?"

84

Research and Inquiry 90
Make Connections 92
Show Your Knowledge 93

Week 2 • Get Up and Go!

Build Knowledge..94

My Goals..96

Literature Big Book *Pouch!*

Respond to the Big Book...98

Main Character..100

Analyze the Text..102

Shared Read "We Can"...104

Paired Selection "Baby Animals on the Move!"

Analyze the Text..110

Shared Read "I Can, We Can"......................................112

Research and Inquiry..118

Make Connections...120

Show Your Knowledge...121

Gary Vestal/Photographer's Choice/Getty Images

Week 3 • Use Your Senses

Build Knowledge 122

My Goals 124

Literature Big Book *Senses at the Seashore*

Respond to the Big Book 126

Topic and Details 128

Analyze the Text 130

Shared Read "Sam Can See" 132

Paired Selection Poetry About Senses

Analyze the Text 138

Shared Read "I Can See" 140

Research and Inquiry 146

Make Connections 148

Show Your Knowledge 149

Think About Your Learning 150

We Are All Readers

Talk about what the children are reading.

 Draw what you like to read about.

We Are All Writers

the sun GUS
Ana
I play ball.
Mei
ABCDEFG
a fish
cat
I see a fox.

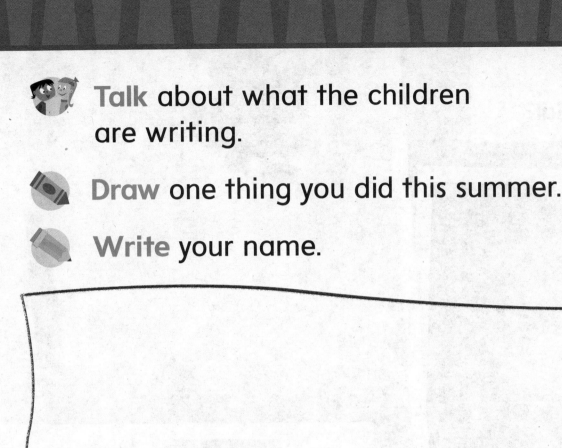 **Talk** about what the children are writing.

Draw one thing you did this summer.

Write your name.

Talk About It

Essential Question

How is everyone special?

Talk about what the children are doing.

 Draw one thing you like to do.

Talk about the story.
How is the gray duckling different?

 Draw how this duckling is different.

Listen to part of the story.

 Talk about the direction
Mother Duck gives her ducklings.

 Say the directions below in order.
Then act them out.

- **Stand up.**
- **Hop.**
- **Sit down.**

NARONGRIT LOKOOLPRAKIT/Shutterstock.com

Find Text Evidence

 Read to find out what makes the children special.

 Circle the letters **A** and **a**.

I Am Special!

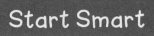

Shared Read

 Talk about what each child is doing.

 Circle the child who is playing with the balls.

Shared Read

 Talk about what the girl on this page is doing.

 Retell the story. Use the pictures to help you.

I Am Special

 Draw a picture of yourself.

 Write your name.

Hello! My name is

_____

- -

_____

Draw what makes you special.

 Say hello and introduce yourself.

 Share your work.

We Are Special **21**

Find Text Evidence

Read to find out what each child does.

Circle and read aloud the word **I**.

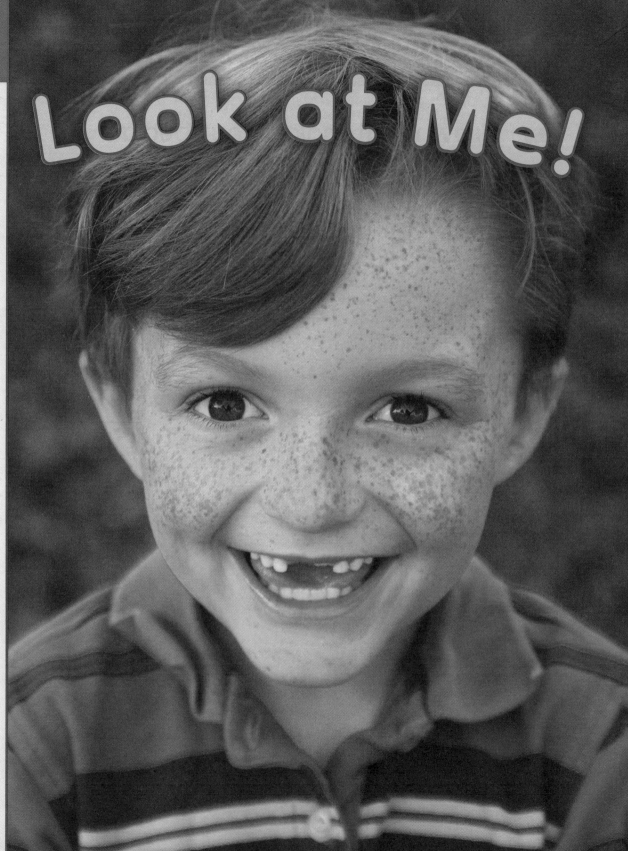

Look at Me!

I .

jump

Shared Read

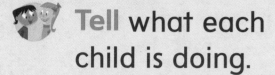 **Tell** what each child is doing.

Circle what the girl needs to help her paint.

I  .

dance

Ariel Skelley/Blend Images

I .

paint

 **Find Text Evidence**

Circle the child who is writing.

Retell the text. Use the words and photos to help you.

I  .

read

I ___ .

write

Talk About It

Talk about what the family is doing.

Draw one thing you do with your family.

Jack Hollingsworth/Photodisc/Getty Images

Talk about the story.
What do the mice do?

 Draw an important part of the story.

Listen to part of the story.

 Talk about what the mice need.

 Write about one thing you may need in school. Then tell your teacher.

I may need

_____

- -

_____

- -

_____

Find Text Evidence

 Read to find out how the family is having fun.

Look at the picture. Tell what each person is doing.

# Family Fun!

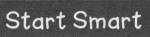

Shared Read

Find Text Evidence

Circle who is preparing food on page 34.

Talk about why they are preparing the food.

Shared Read

🔍 **Find Text Evidence**

Circle the person the cake is for. How do you know?

Retell the story. Use the pictures to help you.

My Family and Me

 Draw a picture of you and your family.

Draw a place you go with your family.

 Say hello and introduce yourself.

 Share your work.

Find Text Evidence

 Read to find out what the family is doing.

 Circle what the boy can pour.

Fun Together!

I can .

pour

 **Find Text Evidence**

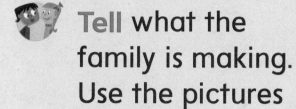 **Tell** what the family is making. Use the pictures to help you.

Circle and read aloud the word **can**.

I can  .

mix

I can .
bake

Shared Read

 **Find Text Evidence**

Circle what the girl can eat. How do you know?

Retell the story. Use the words and pictures to help you.

I can  .
clean

I can  !
eat

Talk about what the girl can do.

 Draw one thing you can do.

Talk about the text.
What can the children do?

 Draw one thing they can do.

Listen to part of the text.

 Talk about what you would like to learn this year. Now listen to what your partner wants to learn.

 Draw what you would like to learn.

Find Text Evidence

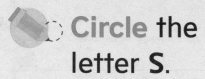 Read to find out what the children can do at school.

 Circle the letter **S**.

At School

Shared Read

 Find Text Evidence

 Think about how the children on this page can take turns talking.

 Tell your ideas to your partner. Take turns talking.

Shared Read

 Talk about what the children are doing on these pages.

 Retell the story. Use the pictures to help you.

I Can!

 Draw one thing you can do at school.

Draw one thing you can do at home.

 Say hello and introduce yourself.

 Share your work.

Find Text Evidence

Read to find out what each child can do.

Listen to the words in the title. Clap for each word.

What Can I Do?

I can .
ride

 **Find Text Evidence**

Talk about what each child can do.

Circle and read aloud the words **I** and **can**.

LWA/Dann Tardif/Blend Images/Getty Images

I can .

rake

I can 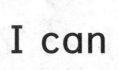 .

walk

Shared Read

Circle what each child likes to read.

Retell the text. Use the words and photos to help you.

Can I  ?
read

I can !
read

Unit 1
Take a New Step

The Big Idea

What can we learn when we try new things?

Say hello to your partner. Say your name, too.

Talk about each photo.

Circle someone in each photo who is trying something new.

FatCamera/E+/Getty Images

Build Knowledge

? Essential Question How can we get along with new friends?

Build Vocabulary

 Talk about getting along with new friends. What words tell about getting along?

 Draw a picture of one of the words.

My Goals

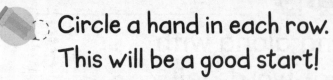
Circle a hand in each row.
This will be a good start!

What I Know Now

I can read and understand texts.

I can write about the texts I read.

I know how to get along with new friends.

Key

 I understand.

 I need more practice.

 I do not understand.

 You will come back to the next page later.

Circle a hand in each row. How did you do?

What I Learned

I can read and understand texts.

I can write about the texts I read.

I know how to get along with new friends.

Retell the story.

 Draw an important part of the story.

 Text Evidence

Page

Talk about ways friends can get along.

 Draw one way friends can get along.

The characters are the people or animals that a made-up story is about.

 Listen to the story.

 Talk about the characters.

 Write who the characters are.

The characters are

_____

- -

_____

_____

- -

_____

Draw the characters. Show something they do.

Look at pages 18–19 and 32–33.

 Talk about how Bear's feelings change.

 Write and **draw** your ideas.

First Bear feels

Then Bear feels

Find Text Evidence

Read to find out what the boy can do.

Read and point to each word in the title.

I Can

I can  the .
see   mitt

 **Find Text Evidence**

Underline and read the word **the**.

Circle an object whose name begins with the same sound as **map**.

I can 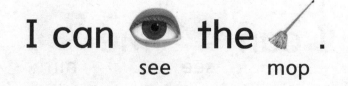 the 🧹.

see   mop

Stockbyte/PunchStock

I can 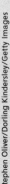 see the drum.

🔍 Find Text Evidence

✏️ **Circle** the things whose names begin with the same sound as **map**.

👧👦 **Retell** the text. Use the photos to help you.

I can 👁 the 🔵.
see   marbles

I can see the broom.

Look at the photos. What are some ways to be a friend?

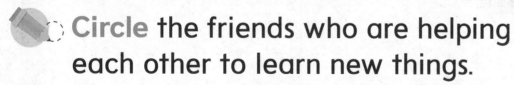 **Circle** the friends who are helping each other to learn new things.

 Draw a box around the friends who are playing a game.

Listen to the list.

 Talk about the directions on the list. When can you use these directions to make a new friend?

1. Say hello.

2. Tell your name.

3. Ask your new friend to play.

 Say the directions on the list in order.

 Act out the directions. Take turns with a partner.

SOCIAL STUDIES

Quick Tip

You can use these sentence starters:

I can use the directions to _____.
I can make friends by _____.

Talk About It

How do the photos in this text show ways to be friends?

Ken Cavanagh/McGraw-Hill Education

Shared Read

 Find Text Evidence

 Read to find out what the girl can do.

 Circle an object whose name begins with the same sound as **mop**.

Can I 👁 the 🗺 ?
see   map

Shared Read

🔍 **Find Text Evidence**

✏️ **Underline** the uppercase letters.

✏️ **Circle** and read the word **the**.

I can.

Can I  the  ?
see · chair

Find Text Evidence

 Circle what the girl can see on this page.

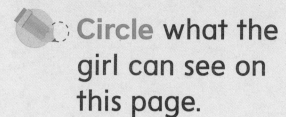 **Retell** the story. Use the pictures to help you.

I can.

I can  !

see   me

How to Be a Good Friend

Step 1 **Talk** about how to be a good friend.

Step 2 **Write** a question about what a good friend might do.

_____

- -

_____

_____

- -

_____

Step 3 **Talk** to classmates. Ask them your question.

Step 4 Draw what you learned.

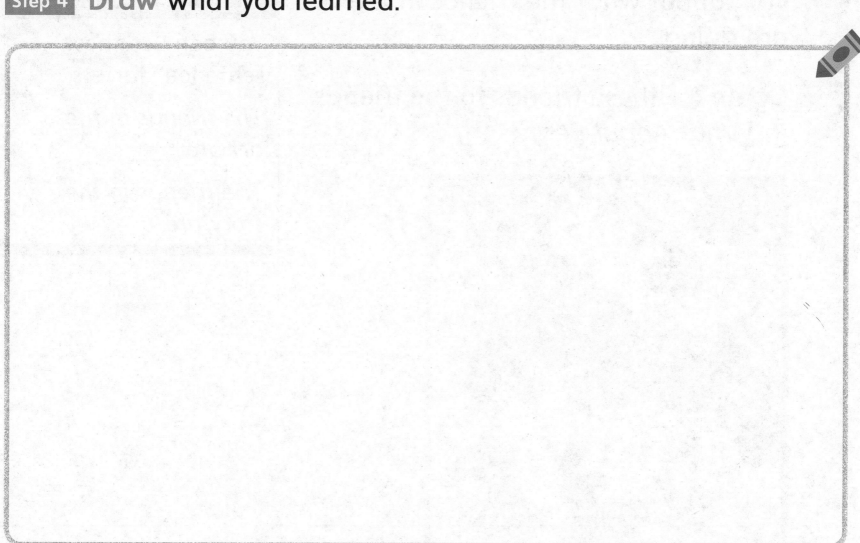

Step 5 Choose a good way to present your work.

Make Connections

 Talk about what the friends in the art are doing.

 Compare these friends to the friends in *What About Bear?*

ImageZoo/SuperStock

Make a Kindness Banner

① **Think** about the texts you read. What did you learn about how to get along with new friends?

② **Talk** about what happens when we are kind to our friends.

③ **Draw** one thing that can happen when we are kind.

Think about what you learned this week. Turn to page 69.

Build Knowledge

Build Vocabulary

 Talk about how baby animals move. What words tell about how baby animals move?

 Draw a picture of one of the words.

Sue Flood/Stone/Getty Images

My Goals

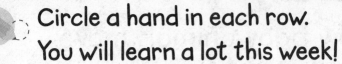 Circle a hand in each row.
You will learn a lot this week!

What I Know Now

I can read and understand texts.

I can write about the texts I read.

I know how baby animals move.

Key

 I understand.

 I need more practice.

 I do not understand.

 You will come back to the next page later.

Circle a hand in each row. You are doing great!

What I Learned

I can read and understand texts.

I can write about the texts I read.

I know how baby animals move.

Retell the story.

 Draw an important part of the story.

 Text Evidence

Page

Talk about how the animals in *Pouch!* move.

 Draw how one of the animals moves.

The **main character** is the person or animal a fiction story is mostly about.

 Listen to the story.

 Talk about the main character.

 Write the name of the main character.

The main character is

_____

- -

_____

- -

_____

Draw the main character.

 Look at page 12. How does the author let you know that Joey is talking?

 Draw and **write** about what Joey wants to do when he says, "Pouch!"

Joey wants to

Look at page 34.

 Talk about what the baby kangaroos mean when they say, "No, thanks."

 Draw what the baby kangaroos want to do.

Find Text Evidence

Read to find out what animals can do.

Circle and read the word **We**.

We Can

Eastphoto/age fotostock

We can .

walk

Shared Read

 Find Text Evidence

Ask questions you may have about the text as you read. This can help you learn information.

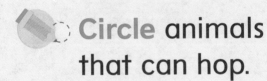 **Circle** animals that can hop.

We can  .

hop

Magdalena Biskup Travel Photography/Flickr/Getty Images

We can  .

climb

Shared Read

🔍 **Find Text Evidence**

✏️ **Underline** words that have the same middle sound as **fan**.

👫 **Retell** the text. Use the photos to help you.

We can .

run

Alan Carey/Corbis

We can .

hug

Paired Selection

 Look at the photos on these pages.
How do different baby animals move?

Mother lion and cubs

Mother duck and ducklings

 Circle the baby animals that
are swimming.

 Draw a box around the baby
animals that are crawling.

Quick Tip

You can use these
sentence starters:

*The lion and cubs
are _____.*

*The duck and
ducklings are _____.*

(l)Comstock Images/Stockbyte/Getty Images; (r)Splinter Images/Alamy

110 Unit 1 • Week 2

Mother horse and foal

Baby turtles

 Talk about how the photos give information about ways baby animals move.

Talk About It

How does the title "Baby Animals on the Move!" help you know what this text is about?

Shared Read

🔍 **Find Text Evidence**

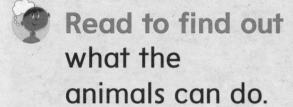

Read to find out what the animals can do.

Underline the lowercase letters in the title.

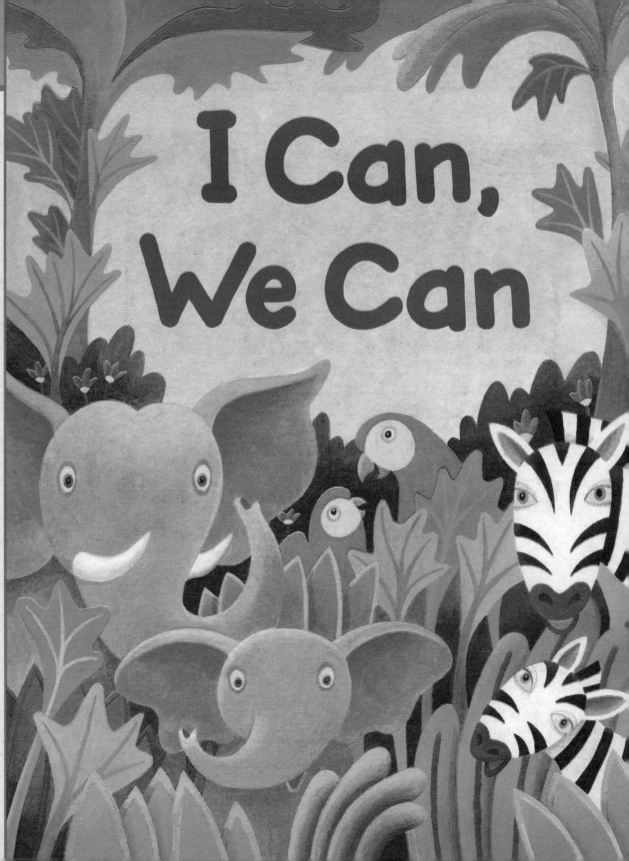

I Can, We Can

I can .
swim

Find Text Evidence

✏ Underline and read the word **We**.

⭕ Circle animals that are in the water.

We can 🐘. swim

I can  .

fly

Shared Read

🔍 **Find Text Evidence**

Circle words that have the same middle sound as **bat**.

Retell the story. Use the pictures to help you.

We can .

fly

116 Unit I • Week 2

We can .

run

Research and Inquiry

How a Baby Animal Moves

Step 1 Talk about ways baby animals move.
Choose one to learn about.

Step 2 Write a question about how
the animal moves.

_____

- -

_____

_____

- -

_____

Step 3 Look at books or use the Internet.

Step 4 Draw what you learned.

Step 5 Choose a good way to present your work.

The Little Bird

I saw a little bird
Come hop, hop, hop.
So I called, "Little bird,
Will you stop, stop, stop?"

I asked the little bird,
"How do you do?"
But it shook its little tail,
And far away it flew.

 Listen to the poem.

 Think about how the little bird moves.

 Compare how the little bird moves to the way Joey moves in *Pouch!*

Quick Tip

You can use these sentence starters:

The little bird can _____.

Joey can _____.

Make a Baby Animals Poster

1 **Think** about the texts you read. What did you learn about how baby animals move?

2 **Choose** one way that baby animals move. **Make** a poster that shows animals that move in this way.

3 **Write** one word that tells how the animals move. Use a word that you learned this week.

Think about what you learned this week. Turn to page 97.

Build Knowledge

Essential Question How can your senses help you learn?

Build Vocabulary

Talk about how you can use your senses to learn. What words tell about the senses?

Draw a picture of one of the words.

My Goals

Circle a hand in each row.
There are no wrong answers!

What I Know Now

I can read and understand texts.

I can write about the texts I read.

I know how my senses help me learn.

Key

 I understand.

 I need more practice.

 I do not understand.

 You will come back to the next page later.

Circle a hand in each row.
Keep working hard!

What I Learned

I can read and understand texts.

I can write about the texts I read.

I know how my senses help me learn.

Retell the text.

 Draw a fact from the text.

Text Evidence

Page

Talk about ways people use their senses.

 Draw one way that people use their senses.

The **topic** is what a nonfiction text is mostly about. Nonfiction has facts and **details** that tell more about the topic.

 Listen to the text.

 Talk about the topic and details.

 Write the topic.

The topic is

_____

- -

_____

_____

_____

- -

_____

Draw one detail.

Listen to and **look** at parts of the text.

 Talk about how your senses help you know what the seashore is like.

 Draw details here.

see	
hear	

Listen to and **look** at pages 24–25.

 Talk about how the words and photos help you know about seaweed.

 Draw and **write** about seaweed.

The seaweed is

_____

- -

_____

Find Text Evidence

 Read to find out what Sam can see.

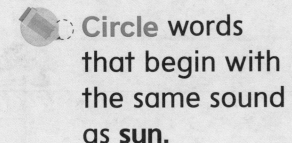 **Circle** words that begin with the same sound as **sun.**

Sam Can See

We can see Sam.

Find Text Evidence

Underline and read the word **see.**

Circle what Sam can see.

We can see the 🐦.

bird

Sam can see the  .

bird

Shared Read

 Ask questions you may have about the story.

 Retell the story. Use the pictures to help you.

Sam can see the .

bird

The  bird can see Sam.

Listen to the poems. Look at the pictures. How do we use our senses to learn?

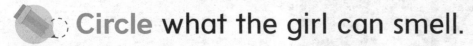 **Circle** what the girl can smell.

 Draw a box around what the woman can taste.

Quick Tip

You can use these sentence starters:

The girl can smell _____.

The woman can taste _____.

Listen to "I Smell Springtime" again.

 Talk about words the author uses in the poem that tell spring is here.

 Draw one way the poem tells that spring is here.

Talk About It

Why are "I Smell Springtime" and "Taste of Purple" good titles for these poems?

🔍 **Find Text Evidence**

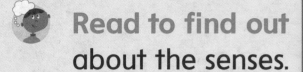

Read to find out about the senses.

⬠ **Circle** and read the word **see**.

I Can See

I can see the .

apple

Find Text Evidence

Circle things whose names begin with the same sound as **am**.

Underline and read the word **can**.

I can .
touch

Don Smith/Alamy

I can .
smell

Shared Read

🔍 **Find Text Evidence**

Circle what helps the girl taste.

Retell the text. Use the photos to help you.

I can .

hear

Danilo Donadoni/Marka/SuperStock

I can .
taste

The Senses

Step 1 Talk about your five senses. Also talk about the body parts that help you use each sense. Choose one sense to learn about.

Step 2 Write a question about this sense.

_____

- -

_____

_____

- -

_____

Step 3 Look at books or use the Internet.

Step 4 Draw what you learned.

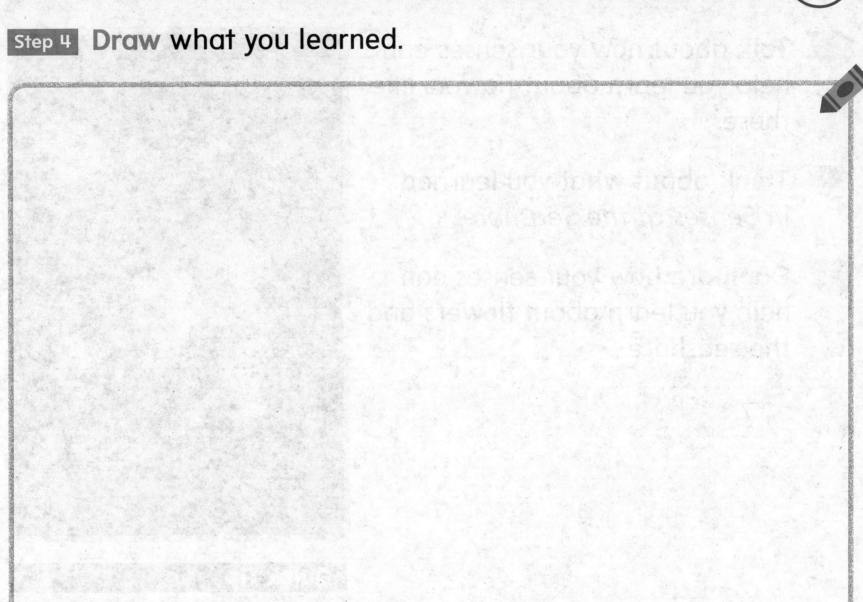

Step 5 Choose a good way to present your work.

Talk about how your senses can help you learn about flowers like these.

 Think about what you learned in *Senses at the Seashore.*

 Compare how your senses can help you learn about flowers and the seashore.

Quick Tip

Use these sentence starters:
My senses help me _____.
In the text, _____.

Make a Senses Book

1. **Think** about the texts you read. What did you learn about how your senses help you learn?

2. **Choose** one sense. **Draw** one way this sense is important.

3. **Write** about why this sense is important. Use a few words that you learned this week.

Think about what you learned this week. Turn to page 125.

Think About Your Learning

Think about what you learned in this unit.

 Share one thing you did well.

 Write one thing you want to get better at.

_____

- - - - - - - - - - - - - - - - -

_____

- - - - - - - - - - - - - - - - -

_____

Share a goal you have with your partner.

My Sound-Spellings

Aa — a — apple	**Bb** — b — bat	**Cc** — c ck k — camel	**Dd** — d — dolphin	**Ee** — e — egg	**Ff** — f — fire	**Gg** — g — guitar
Hh — h_ — hippo	**Ii** — i — insect	**Jj** — j — jump	**Kk** — c k ck — koala	**Ll** — l — lemon	**Mm** — m — map	**Nn** — n — nest
Oo — o — octopus	**Pp** — p — piano	**Qq** — qu_ — queen	**Rr** — r — rose	**Ss** — s — sun	**Tt** — t — turtle	**Uu** — u — umbrella
Vv — v — volcano	**Ww** — w_ — window	**Xx** — x — box	**Yy** — y_ — yo-yo	**Zz** — z _s — zipper		

Aa Bb Cc Dd Ee

Ff Gg Hh Ii Jj

Kk Ll Mm Nn

Oo Pp Qq Rr

Ss Tt Uu Vv

Ww Xx Yy Zz